This book is dedicated to all the tenacious transmuters of the past and to the ones of the future.

"Then I was standing on the highest Mountain of them all, and round about beneath me was the whole hoop of the world. And while I stood there I saw more than I can tell and I understood more than I saw; for I was seeing in a sacred manner the shapes of all things in the spirit, and the shape of all shapes as they must live together as one being. And I saw that the sacred hoop of my people was one of many hoops that made one circle, wide as daylight and as starlight, and in the centre grew one mighty flowering tree to shelter all the children of one mother and one father. And I saw that it was holy"

Black Elk

The Body Electronics Experience
Author's Note

This booklet is an introductory guide to the principles and preparations necessary for optimum results within the practice of Body Electronics Pointholding Intensives held by Illia. Body Electronics is a wholistic self-healing modality. It requires dedicated efforts in self education, nutritional preparations, as well as a deep commitment to one's own healing and service to humankind.

- How We Heal, by Douglas Morrison -in print
- Logic In Sequence Book 1-
- The Laws of Perfection by John Whitman Ray, founder of Body Electronics
- Logic In Sequence Book 2- The Healing Crisis
- Logic In Sequence Book 3- The Electrification Of Matter

How We Heal may be ordered through your local bookstore, LIS are out of publication, but may be found in full free of charge on my site. I include quotes or pages from the above books for you to refer. May this little book serve to guide and inspire further research and application of wholistic principles and natural law.

In no way is the content of this book meant to prescribe, diagnose or treat any medical condition. Consult your medical professionals.

Dr. John Whitman Ray (1934-2001) founded and developed what is now known as Body Electronics. John began with study, research and experimentation accompanied by pure intent (service to humankind) visionary experience and prayer. This was his life's work.

Today Body Electronics continues to offer a community based, wholistic self- healing practice. This modality is unparalleled. Based in natura law, participants learn the importance of physical principles that include a nutritional foundation to springboard emotional evolution.

Trauma is gradually released through a sequential process that includes sustained acupressure called 'pointholding'.

With the guidance of a certified Body Electronics instructor, one learns how to both apply the techniques and receive equally. When appropriately applied, consciousness change is a pleasant side effect.

To Whom It May Concern;

Illia has been studying Body Electronics with great dedication since attending her first BE seminar in January 2002. Over the next four years, Illia attended over forty weeks of BE seminars with me. This included attendance at two complete BE Instructors seminars of five weeks duration each, as well as numerous BE Intensives. At my invitation, Illia has also helped me teach several BE Intensives. At these, Illia did a fine job, both with the lecture portion as well as the pointholding.

Illia has also been active for the past few years teaching BE seminars to enthusiastic participants internationally.

Illia also attended the four week Visualization & Consciousness seminar in 2005. While in attendance at this advanced seminar, Illia had the experience of reaching zero ohms resistance, as measured by a sensitive galvanometer, a total of four times. This took place over two days, and was witnessed by two separate facilitators. This is a significant milestone that has, to my knowledge, been reached by only a handful of people involved with BE over the years.

 For those interested in learning Body Electronics under the expert guidance of a dedicated and compassionate instructor, allow me to highly recommend that you study with Illia Heart.

Yours in Health,

Douglas W. Morrison New Cumberland, Pennsylvania October 1, 2006

☆Douglas Morrison and Illia Heart after the completion of the Visualization and Consciousness Course-2005

"UNTIL MAN CAN EXPERIENCE ON THE MENTAL LEVEL THAT WHICH EXISTS ON THE PHYSICAL LEVEL, HE WILL BE BOUND TO THE PHYSICAL." JWR~

~True Healing~

'THE ONLY TRUE HEALING ON THE PHYSICAL BODY
TAKES PLACE WHEN A CHANGE OF CONSCIOUSNESS
OCCURS. FOR A CHANGE OF CONSCIOUSNESS TO OCCUR
IT IS NECESSARY TO VISUALIZE THE THOUGHTS
(SENSORY EXPERIENCE), FEELINGS (EMOTIONS), AND
WORD PATTERN (VERBAL AND INTERNAL), ON THE
MENTAL LEVEL, THAT THEY MAY BE RE-EXPERIENCED
AND RELEASED AS A PATTERN OF ENERGY THUS
FREEING ONE'S SELF OF THE CONTINUATION OF
SUPPRESSED THOUGHTS, FEELINGS, AND WORD THAT
THE OUTER MANIFESTATION OF DISEASE MAY BE
RELEASED THAT THE PERFECT PATTERN OF DNA MAY
THEN BE MANIFEST. AN UNDERSTANDING OF THE
ABOVE LAW MUST BE UNDERSTOOD AND APPLIED THAT
YOU MAY FREE YOURSELF OF BONDAGE OF YOUR OWN
CREATION. ALL BODY BALANCING TECHNIQUES WHICH
DO NOT EMBODY THE ABOVE INFORMATION ARE
TEMPORARY IN THEIR EFFECTS AT BEST AND DO NOT
BRING ABOUT TRUE HEALING. TO MOVE BEYOND MERE
BALANCING AND INTO ACTUAL REGENERATION, WE
MUST EFFECT A CHANGE OF CONSCIOUSNESS. THE
SOURCE OF ALL DISEASE (WHICH IS AFTER ALL OUR OWN
INNER CREATIVE ESSENCE OF THOUGHT FEELING AND
WORD) MUST BE REEXPERIENCED ON THE MENTAL
LEVEL THAT THE PHYSICAL BONDAGE VIA OUR SELF
IMPOSED REACTIVE MECHANISMS MAY THEN DROP
AWAY.
     SUCH IS THE PATH TO ASCENSION.' JWR

TWELVE POINTS ON BODY ELECTRONICS
Introduction for Beginners
by Dr. John Whitman Ray, N.D., N.M.D.

"Contempt prior to complete investigation will enslave a man to ignorance."   Anonymous

The following is a guide to aid the individual to understand the basic concepts of Body Electronics with the express intent that the most favourable results be obtained in the time expended. The individual is encouraged to maintain a persistent and consistent course of activity in Body Electronics, that the desired benefits (side effects of consciousness change) of physical health, emotional well being and peace of mind may be eventually obtained. Ponder and pray upon each of the following concepts as it is necessary to understand and apply each of them that Body Electronics may be effective and not relegated to a mechanical method played upon the physical body.

1. Body Electronics, when properly applied, is done in a quiet, loving atmosphere, permeated with gentleness and patience, with commitment on the part of all concerned to professionalism and confidentiality, and encompassed with mutual trust,

concern and discretion. Body Electronics is applied in an exact, systematic, methodical manner, which should rarely be deviated from in order to obtain satisfactory and lasting results.

Body Electronics is in part a method of sustained acupressure, which requires an understanding of nutritional preparation, anatomical structure, physiological function, emotional interactivity, and mental processes within a framework of what is known as the "Healing Crisis."

2. Body Electronics requires an understanding of the "Healing Crisis."

Hering's Law of Cure has been accepted for many years as the basic underlying definition of the "healing Crisis." This concept has been accepted by Natural Health Practitioners the world over including Chiropractic Physicians, Naturopathic Physicians, Homeopathic Physicians, Herbalists, Iridologists and a host of other valid natural healing modalities.

HERING'S LAW OF CURE

"All 'cure' starts from within out and from the head down and in reverse order as the symptoms have appeared."

Since the introduction of Body Electronics to the world, a new explanation concerning the "Healing Crisis" has been necessary.

THE LAW OF HEALING CRISIS -- JOHN WHITMAN RAY

"A healing crisis will occur only when an individual is ready both physiologically and psychologically (and spiritually). The basic foundation for healing crisis is nutritional preparedness. A healing crisis (cure) will begin from within out, in reverse order chronologically as to how the symptoms have appeared, tempered by the intensity of the trauma. The individual will have the opportunity to re-experience (and release) each trauma, both physiological and psychological, beginning with the trauma of least severity (whatever we are ready and willing to process in that moment of time). It must be recognized that traumas involving emotions, which include all traumas, will be released in order beginning with unconsciousness, then apathy, grief, fear, anger, pain and eventually enthusiasm (love), in conjunction with the appropriate word patterns for each emotion and thought patterns (sensory memory) which are accessible at each level. Unconditional love and unconditional forgiveness are the keys to apply to transmute any resistance at any level once these resistances are brought to view through the application of the Laws of Love, Light and Perfection.

Amplification of the above concept is found in Book One of the "Logic in Sequence" series.

3. Body Electronics can best be explained initially by a physical demonstration in the physics laboratory. When a crystal is compressed it emits an energy and/or electric current, which can be measured by sensitive instrumentation. This energy or electrical current is known as the piezoelectric effect. In the human body there are formations of crystals in various acupressure points or reflex points or along the spine and elsewhere in the physical body. These crystals or calcifications are found within joints or in injury throughout the body and in the cranial sutures. As each crystal is compressed using specific Body Electronics technology, the crystal slowly dissolves and releases an energy, which can be experienced by the pointholder as well as the pointholdee. These energies will be explained in point twelve.
In Body Electronics, the pointholdee may have one or more pointholders. One person among the pointholders is appointed or chosen by the pointholdee to be a facilitator who will inquire from

time to time as to what is happening (being accessed). One who is the facilitator will encourage the pointholdee (with intuition) to re-experience on the mental level all memories that present themselves and traumas as if they were occurring in the everpresent now.

One and a half to two hours is the average time but there are exceptions. If pointholding is open ended it relieves one of stress or anxiety concerning time limits. Thus, one can relax and pay close attention to the "healing crisis" as it evolves. This open ended time element makes it difficult for professionals engaged in the healing arts to plan organized appointments. Therefore, the success of a good pointholding program is dependent upon people helping people rather than depending on a "therapist" from any existing healing modality. People must learn to be individually responsible and learn to help themselves.

An atmosphere of joy and enthusiasm is desirable to be maintained during pointholding but not to the degree of distracting the individual from placing attention on the traumas and resistances, which appear to the consciousness of the pointholdee as the crystal is in the process of dissolving. It must be understood that the pointholder may be going through a healing crisis while one is "holding" points. This should be handled in a like manner until the pointholding is complete and the healing crisis is over.

Let us now consider the concept of the everpresent now. The understanding of the everpresent now is a difficult concept for some to accept or understand due to the fact that all mankind to one degree or another is caught up in the lifestream of continual activity, which traps the attention of the individual.

This catching of the attention by outer activity can be thought of as trapped attention wherein one ceases to recognize that all outer activity is the outer manifestation of inner essence. With this in mind after pondering and prayer the candid and reflective mind will begin to understand the healing crisis as the body mechanism begins to repair itself through the change of consciousness of the individual. Thought is senior to substance. Substance does not construct thought as substance is present for the purpose of being acted upon by intelligence. Thought controls and determines the structure of substance. One will eventually understand that the only creative forces in the universe are thought (sensory experience), feelings (emotionality) and the spoken word (verbal expressions in word and thought). These three, thought, feeling and spoken word we must learn how to master.

The mastery of Body Electronics in its fullest expression encompasses the Laws of Love, Light and Perfection, which are explained in the Logic in Sequence Series. This is one path an individual may choose to follow on the pathway of individual self-realization or enlightenment. Nothing is ever gained without spiritual seeking which is a distinct mental attitude composed of will and determination -- a focused intent. Nothing is ever gained without a specific asking, which is a direct verbal request for that which one desires from a spiritual source. Nothing is ever obtained without knocking, which is a physical act of doing all one can do to keep those laws and principles of a universal nature which give life and light to the physical body. These laws and principles are the laws of God. Faith and belief is not enough. Faith without works is dead. Faith without appropriate obedience to natural law is to no avail. The facilitator must never ask a person why. In reality one does not really know why one reacts. The question "why?" is meaningless and therefore must be deleted from meaningful questioning or responsible guidance. The conscious mind can manufacture a multitude of of reasons or justifications why one did something but the simplicity of the entire matter is that a reaction stems from suppressed programming which may even be a genetic inheritance. Ask the individual what is happening now, where is it happening, when is it happening? Work within a framework of reality and certainty in this life, with this body and do not encourage one to put one's attention on speculation or fantasy.

All that is necessary to master is in this life now. Please remember that the avoidance of reality is disguised in a number of ways. The facilitator should always encourage the pointholdee to re-experience all traumas or experience in the everpresent now since all memories were at one time experienced in the everpresent now, and they were resisted in the everpresent now. The facilitator must remember that he/she is not the psychiatrist who probes. The facilitator encourages the pointholdee to be discrete and to discipline oneself to experience all things on the mental level while disciplining the physical body by holding the body still. The facilitator should encourage/remind one to hold still and to breath deep and regular. One must be patient, kind and gentle regarding these matters as one is not immediately the epitome of self-discipline and it will take some time to learn to master these things. One must remember that little is gained by venting one's emotion and to reactively flip and flop around like a fish out of water. To be productive as one will learn from experience, all these emotions and memories must be experienced on the mental level within a framework of self-discipline of body, emotions and mind. It must be stressed that some people are unstable and should not participate with Body Electronics. Do not be too quick to help an individual until you have some understanding of their past. If they are on medication, leave them on that medication and under no circumstances remove them from that medication but let the need be ascertained by the Medical practitioner who is skilled in his field. Remember: Overzealousness must be tempered with caution and wisdom. Know the nature of the individual you desire to serve.

4. In the human body a "crystal" or calcification can be compared to a computer chip or microchip. In reality, a crystal in the human body is an "organic computer chip" full of stored memory. This memory is gradually released which is then re-experienced by the individual, which is called healing crisis. Healing

crisis has been defined in point two. This suppressed memory can be the result of physical or emotional trauma wherein resistance to an experience of life has occured. If these crystals are genetically inherited then they will have some form of genetic memory stored within the crystal. A sustained pressure is exerted in a specific manner during this entire process until it is complete. This shall briefly be described later. Regarding the sustained acupressure, one should first of all be sure that the fingernails are clippped short (and filed) as not to penetrate the skin during pointholding. The pain from a fingernail is unnecessary and distracting and can be damaging to the skin. The hands should be washed and clean prior to pointholding. If a body part is without innervation or is numb one may not feel pain, thus heavy acupressure will not be productive and one may unknowingly traumatize the tissue under heavy pressure. Common sense and communication is important. One should keep the pressure sustained on the point that one can be kept on the brink of being able to lovingly and willingly endure the pain. Remember: One is not causing pain when pressing gently on a pressure point, one is releasing carefully the suppressed pain which is encoded in the crystal.

When one lovingly and willingly endures the pain in a given area of concern; all anger, fear, grief, apathy, and unconsciousness are rapidly transmuted by the pain, while the pain is being transmuted by loving enthusiasm. It's important to note that one realize while applying pressure on the point that the pointholdee may not feel the numbness, pain, heat, cold, electricity, throbbing, etc., immediately.

5. It is imperative to learn that one of the prime prerequisites to effective Body Electronics is to learn to "Lovingly and Willingly Endure all of the Experiences of Life." One must be constantly aware of what is transpiring in one's life and to look for the lesson to be learned from the universe as one patiently experiences each activity of life with non-resistance and with the spirit of unlimited gratitude. One must learn to release all patterns of resistances such as old grudges and hard feelings with unconditional love and unconditional forgiveness, knowing that for the most part that people do what they are programmed to do and have very little free agency to overcome this programming that they may conduct their life in a different manner. Once we understand this we can freely forgive people for what they have done because, in essence, they really do not have a clear perception

as to why they do what they do. For the most part we are all creatures of reaction and are delightful deviations from the norm.

6. In reference to point five, it is therefore always appropriate that all pointholders and pointholdees be reminded that one must never allow judgment, criticism, or condemnation to enter one's mind toward any other person or thing. We must all learn that what we resist in life will be drawn to us with computer like precision. If we inspect carefully our inner thoughts, putting all self-justification aside for how we act or react, we will find within ourselves the very faults, which we are so quick to see in others. The faults we see in others which attract our attention should be an immediate signal to go inside and search for the error in our own thinking. This is appropriate instruction for both pointholders and pointholdees. Without question it is a difficult job to apply this instruction, yet it is far better to be the master of one's self than to conquer an enemy on the battlefield of war.

7. To fully understand the depth of effectiveness that Body Electronics is capable of attaining one must learn to understand the following principle:

"Until man can experience on the mental level that which exists on the physical level, he will be bound to the physical."

This is explained in depth in Chapter One of Book One of the Logic in Sequence Series. What exactly does Body Electronics do? It begins by restoring the nerve supply to the body, which enables a restoration of communication to take place between the cell and the brain. When the nerve supply is restored, then circulation to the body part affected is restored. When the circulation is restored, then the nutrient saturation necessary for bodily regeneration can reach the cells and tissues. Toxins are flushed out of the cells and the cells regain their normal function, after a "healing crisis" is experienced by the individual.

Prior to Body Electronics application, which is called pointholding, one can examine the pain threshold of the pointholdee by a gentle "pinch test." A high pain threshold indicates a degree of ennervation or lack of nerve supply. As Body Electronics is applied there will exist a restoration of nerve supply, which can be evidenced by greater sensitivity or a lower pain threshold when the pinch test is applied. A low pain threshold indicating the ability to "feel" is now restored to the individual, which is a desired state as it always precedes healing or regeneration of the body.

8. In order to understand the necessity of the application of individual responsibility to one's life as one has increased memory and awareness as a result of Body Electronics, one must learn to appropriately apply the "List" to one's life. The explanation of the "List" is thoroughly explained in Chapter Eleven of Book One in the Logic in Sequence Series.
After pointholding there is much that has not been brought to a person's awareness, which should be reflected in the "List." The List requires constant change and revision as one works diligently toward the completion of each item on the List. Remember: We always work from simple to complex, from easy to difficult, wherein each item when completed should be acknowledged before progression to the next item on the List.

9. A requirement for the effective application of Body Electronics will be a specially designed nutritional program as determined by the Iris-Sclera Integrated Diagnosis as designed and taught by John Whitman Ray. This diagnostic procedure will include an appropriate herbal and nutritional supplementation program as well as a defined program for the

application of Body Electronics. This may be sought from a Certified Body Electronics Instructor.

It is imperative to understand that a nutrient saturation program is essential for Body Electronics to be effective. When Body Electronics is effective, eventually, usually after several pointholdings one may experience a burning searing pain. At this time one is encouraged to breath into the pain deep and regularly as one is holding the body still. `One is reminded to Lovingly and Willingly Endure the Pain with gratitude and enthusiasm. The enthusiasm gradually transmutes the pain in which in turn transmutes the suppressed anger, fear, grief, apathy and unconsciousness. Once the emotional body is transmuted one then is capable of having access to the mental body and can then discern in the area of transmuted emotionality free from the bondage of emotional reaction.

10. It is important to understand that as the crystal or calcification dissolves under the influence of the sustained acupressure, the encoded sensory experience, verbal expression, and emotionality that has been suppressed subtly or dramatically during trauma and which has been encoded or recorded in the crystal or calcification will arise to the

consciousness of the individual to be mentally re-experienced. The sustained acupressure is non-traumatic, non-invasive and when applied appropriately, releases a hologram of sensory experience, verbal expressions, and gradient emotionality, which is released in the following order: Unconsciousness or numbness, apathy, grief, fear, anger, pain and enthusiasm. It must be understood that anything resisted forms a suppressed composite energy pattern, which causes a distortion in the morphogenetic field resulting in a corresponding eventual crystallization in body tissues, which have a similar resonant frequency to the suppressed hologram. The composite wave of energy from the suppressed thought, feeling and spoken word is eventually encoded in the crystal which then becomes the outer manifestation of the inner consciousness.

11. Sustained acupressure is applied in a manner, which is organized, prioritized, and sequentially designated as seen on the flow sheet.

If the procedure is followed patiently and systematically then the encoded sensory experience, verbal expressions and emotionality recorded within the crystal will arise to the consciousness of the individual to be mentally re-experienced. As one goes through consciousness change, the iris fibre structure may change in the corresponding indicated areas. One will see pigment change wherein brown will gradually change to blue, even dark pigment spots will lighten, decrease in size and eventually vanish from the iris. One will see specific iris markings gradually move toward the perfection of iris configuration, free from structural distortions. One will also see significant sclera markings undergo dramatic change. Remember: The eye (Iris and Sclera) is the window to the soul.

12. As the resistances are re-experienced and the sequential emotionality is released, one then moves gradually from the entrapment of the emotional body into the mental body where discernment can occur. Discernment cannot occur when one is dominated by reactive emotionality. With discernment one is then capable of gradually encompassing a series of ever increasing subtle dualities with impartiality and equanimity, releasing each time the identification with one end of the existing duality. At this time the body will experience the vibration of regeneration as the duality is encompassed. The physical body is now renewing or regenerating. The body regains its elasticity, the spinal calcifications disappear and the

middle age prime returns. All of this can only take place as one assumes responsibility for life and corrects or amends on the physical level for all human discord that is out of harmony with unconditional love and unconditional forgiveness.

The pointholder who holds the designated point as part of a prioritized sequence will continually sustain the pressure on the point without moving or changing fingers and will experience one or all of the following: Numbness, pain, electricity, tingling, throbbing or pulsing, heat, coldness or burning.

When all of these are completed the point is "flat" and the fingers will be as they were when first placed on the point. At this point the application of Body Electronics can come to a satisfactory end for that session. If a systematic, non-varying cycling occurs such as heat to cool, cool to heat, heat to cool, cool to heat, etc. this is an indication that one has reached a point where the mineral supply of the body is exhausted and no further progress can be made with the dissolution of the crystals or calcifications. At this time the activity comes to an end with the admonition to increase the necessary nutrients and especially the mineral intake. Provisions are made to complete the same points another time where pointholding can resume where it left off. The experience of cycling is common and is often found where nutrient saturation is not being carefully followed.Record should be made by the pointholdee, of points held with the date and notes which are pertinent to the session (word pattern etc.) should be required to jog further memory. The pointholders consult a chart of sequential points and proceed in order with variation as determined by indicated priorities. The facilitator instructs the pointholdee to hold the body still and breathe deeply while experiencing whatever comes to the awareness. All is experienced with unconditional love and forgiveness. One person (pointholder) is capable of holding points with excellent results. There are occasions when it is preferable for one person to hold one specified point, such as found in Cranial Electronics. The mechanics of the process involved cannot be adequately explained here, as it is experiential rather than intellectual in its scope. Once one experiences the process then one will understand, wherein all the words in the world cannot explain the process as one grasps the causative factors of the inner essence. It is like trying to capture a wisp of wind in the hand and trying to preserve it forever, it cannot be done. As we grasp and apply the fundamentals we eventually self-realize that the physical body and the environment around us reflects our inner consciousness. Body Electronics in its advanced application of specific principles helps one to free himself from the self-imposed shackles from which one has been unable to escape. One must first of all learn the application of unconditional love and unconditional forgiveness with non-resistance to all of the experiences of life and to be grateful for all that the universe serves up on our plate. Through the teachings of Body Electronics, it is imperative to recognize that we will eventually understand that we have drawn to ourselves by the law of attraction all that which we have resisted. Every thought is meaningful. We reap what we have sown, therefore we must be careful of every thought, word and deed. We now have the opportunity to undo all of our indiscretions and place ourselves by choice, in harmony with Universal Law. As love encompasses all emotionality, allowing the transmutation of the resisted thought, feeling and spoken word, we observe a profound effect on the morphogenetic field. The morphogenetic field is determined by thought and in turn determines the structure of the body and of all living things and the structure of the universe itself. When this love transmutes all resistance on the level of emotionality, then there is a morphogenetic field change and the DNA of the body changes. At the same time all related DNA substance goes through a corresponding change. The human body and related bodies experience profound change through what is known as a "Healing Crisis" which results in a transmutation of disease symptoms. Thus the human body returns to its perfect DNA form as expressed in the prime of life. The physical body is the doorway to spirituality. As we master and discipline the physical, according to the Laws of Love, Light and Perfection, which is the first step, we then progress to the discipline and mastery of the emotional body and finally the mental body, in that order. As this unfolds the outer degenerative conditions of aging and disease gradually disappear and the perfection of the perfect DNA emerges.

Each of you are now invited to discover yourself, from the inside out.

John Whitman Ray

Artist- Kahlil Gibran, Author of The Prophet

Physical and Psychological Preparation

Nutrition~ Stillness~ Breath~ Study

Body Electronics is the practice of lower law, increasing self-mastery as we continue to gain access to higher law. We are building upon lower law, and this requires increasing application. Be aware of reactive patterns with food. Before, during and after a pointholding event, it is especially necessary to give the body support by eating fresh, organic, raw  and nutrient dense food that supports the healing crisis, avoiding substance that inhibits healing crisis such as sugars (glucose and hi-fructose corn products), caffeine, alcohol, recreational drugs, heavy carbohydrates, the list goes on. Drink sufficient amounts of pure spring water while on the nutritional program to flush toxins. Lower law is the foundation to higher law. With that said, be aware of reactive patterns that make physical law the main focus to the exclusion of higher law.

Nutritional Supplementation
Basic requirements for Pointholding

- Build to saturation level gradually prior to pointholding, reduce gradually to maintenance leve after pointholding (minimum 6 weeks before and after).
- Remember the principle, what helps get you into a healing crisis, will support you to get you through the H.C.

This applies to the nutritional program, as well as conscious application of principles.
(How We Heal pg. 369-The Role of Consciousness)
Read- Twelve points on all the following nutrients: www.howweheal.com
For liquid minerals, mineral caps, superfood enzymes, lymphatic enzymes and more see:
www.enzymesinternational.com
The nutritional program will begin to break up suppressed crystals, bringing forth the onset of HC.

1. Superfood Enzymes & Lymphatic Enzymes (EI)

Enzymes- Raw Protein/Amino Acids

These three work interdependently within the body. Enzymes are necessary for digestion and assimilation of nutrients, carbohydrates/sugars, fats and proteins. Raw protein digested efficiently provides the nutritional profile for the production of nine essential amino acids. When provided, the other nonessential amino acids may be synthesized within the body. This provides the endocrine system the necessary nutrition for the production of hormones. When stress is put on one endocrine gland (through hormone imbalance or stress), the effects are felt throughout the system, effecting hormonal production and distribution. The modern diet may consist of a bombardment of sugars, fats etc., where our pancreas is under constant stress to provide necessary enzymes. Supplementation of high quality enzymes may assist to ease this digestive stress, eventually allowing for physical regeneration.

- Enzymes and raw protein provide the nutrition for the formation of amino acids, precursor to hormone production.

- Protein does not perform its function unless broken down into amino acids. Hence the importance of sufficient enzyme activity. Enzymes help extract chelated minerals from food. Enzymes transform chelated minerals into an alkaline detoxifying agent which combines with acid cellular wastes and toxic settlements within the body assisting to neutralize, preparing them for elimination.

- Raw bee pollen- preferably from a local apiary. (digestion is made efficient by crushing and taken with a little honey). Many bean/lentil/ sprouts are good sources of raw protein.

  - Two of 9 essential amino acids, tryptophan and lysine, are destroyed by heating/cooking. Proteins, sugars and fats may require supplemented enzymes to digest efficiently. Hormones act within the body as a catalyst in every metabolic function, endothermic and exothermic reactions which are necessary for biological transmutation; to heal and regenerate tissues and to warm or cool the body (healthy thyroid function).

2. Colloidal Mineral caps and Colloidal Liquid Minerals (Enzymes International).

This informal letter of explanation has been requested by many on the subject of minerals. There is so much that needs to be said that a book of explanation is necessary and could be written on the subject. So please accept this partial but, hopefully, helpful explanation to the inquisitive mind.

(1) The first complaint, which continually reaches my ears, is that large doses of minerals are toxic. This is certainly true in proper perspective. I have no argument against this complaint if the minerals are in a noncolloidal or non-chelated form. The body cannot handle these forms of minerals except in only very small amounts. Those minerals that the body cannot handle settle out in the weakened areas of the body causing toxic settlements. This is seen in the eye as pigmentation spots in the area of the iris which corresponds with that particular weakened organ in the

body. It might be wise to point out that if the toxic material in that particular weakened organ remained there, eventually metabolic breakdown would occur, These undesirable minerals come from hard water, sea water, mineral water, mineral tablets, volcanic ash, etc. According to many nutritional experts, colloidal minerals are nontoxic. It is common knowledge that chelated minerals are certainly nontoxic, as they are necessary for every biochemical function of the body, Chelated minerals are found in the food we eat provided it is grown organically, on land free from synthetic fertilizers and petrochemicals, where it has sufficient mineral content to sustain life.

(2) The next complaint concerns the high amount of sulfur in the Coenzyme Minerals. Sulfur is acknowledged to be toxic in its elemental form. Sulfur dioxide which is made from crude oil and used to prevent darkening of some dried fruits, such as apricots raisins, prune and apples, has been recognized by some experts to damage enzymes. Since it comes from crude oil it has been labeled as a hydrocarbon, a substance often incriminated in cancer.

Toxic effects of sulfur in popular antibiotics have been acknowledged and, for the most part, phased out,. Sulfuric acid, containing sulfur found in coal smoke, smog and exhausts of some large industries is highly corrosive and is believed to be a strong factor in lung cancer. Yet, colloidal sulfur is looked upon internationally as useful and as a safe, effective treatment for arthritis with no contraindications. Colloidal sulfur is an important element in many amino acids. Sulfur has been called the beauty mineral because hair, skin and nails are good storage depots for sulfur. If there is a sulfur deficiency .one can get psoriasis, itchy eczema, rashes and hair may grow slowly or fall out easily. Hair may gray and lose its natural color due to sulfur deficiency. This sulfur has to be in the form of a colloidal, chelated mineral which is what we have in the Coenzyme Mineral solution.

I might add, colloidal sulfur has been used in large amounts by Dr. Edward Karl of Mexico along with the herb, chaparral, as a cleanser of intestinal parasites. So much for sulfur; I trust this will answer that question.

(3) The next complaint is a most vocal and contagious complaint due to partial knowledge. A little knowledge is a very dangerous thing. This complaint is due to the high aluminum content in the Coenzyme Minerals. Everyone knows that a non-colloidal, non-chelated aluminum is toxic to the body. This is an accepted fact; but when the Coenzyme Mineral solution has aluminum in a colloidal, chelated form, it then reveals one of the major secrets behind the simultaneous

cleansing and building of these unique minerals.
The concept of **Dr. Louis Kervran** established on the
last page of his book, Biological Transmutations,
confirms that this form of aluminum is transmuted "in
vitro" in the body to silica and then to calcium.
Everyone knows the importance of silica and calcium to
the establishment of health, but how many know that
colloidal, chelated aluminum will help fulfill many
bodily needs in the great atomic reactor, our body?
(4) To my knowledge, there is no mineral supplement
which will compare in changing the pigmentation in the
eye from brown to blue, provided the enzyme deficiency
is corrected in the body. The removal from the iris of
the eye of radii solaris, pigmentation spots, closed
lesions or lacunae, cholesterol rings and the lymphatic
rosary are unparalleled. The change in the level of the
fiber structure in the iris of the eye, reflecting healing
and regeneration of tissue in the body, is of paramount
and unsurpassed importance.
(5) How can I impress upon you the importance of the
necessity of proper electrolytes to be used to cleanse
and rebuild the body and to maintain sufficient
electrolytes, not used up in the metabolic process, so
that Body Electronics will work? Body Electronics is the
greatest breakthrough of the century in the healing arts.
Without the proper electrolytes in saturation amounts,

the Body Electronics will not work effectively.

(6) These particular minerals have been tested by countless means in all the healing arts; used orally, rectally, intravenously in animals, used externally, internally, large amounts and small amounts with no contraindications.

(7) These minerals have a track record of 60 years commercially and go back to the Indians of pioneer time and before. The Indians used this water in a mud to help heal their wounds. The processing technique used to extract these organic minerals is effective, unique and found nowhere else.

(8) We have found nothing to be as effective in helping to heal burns, scars, inflammations and restore activity to inactive tissues. The health scientists of today and tomorrow will be looking at colloidal electrolytes in proper perspective as one of the major secrets to health, provided the colloidal electrolytes contain the broad range of necessary trace minerals~

(9) Non-chelated trace minerals, hard water, sea water, volcanic ash water, mineral water, etc., etc., etc., have not yet proven to hold a candle to colloidal, chelated minerals in the most p~f~t balance known to man.

(10) When subjected to a tire assay to determine mineral content, the organic nature of the Coenzyme Minerals is destroyed and results are nil.

(11) When these Coenzyme Minerals are heated above 200° F. they begin to be destroyed in their effectiveness because they begin to lose their organic nature.

(12) Freezing will in no way affect the value of the minerals. A flaking due to freezing should be saved to sprinkle on food.

(13) These minerals are tested so they are always the same strength. However, due to their organic nature, it is impossible to keep the color consistent. You will also find that a little "mother" will sometimes form in the minerals much like you find in vinegar. This will not in any way harm the minerals, Remember, these minerals are organic and are sensitive to light, heat and life.

(14) One tablespoon of Coenzyme Minerals is equivalent to approximately 250 mg. of any organic, colloidal, chelated mineral.

(15) A colloidal substance is one substance, or a mixture of substances, in which the particles in the colloidal system are smaller than one milLimicron in diameter. One or many substances called the dispersed phase or colloid is uniformly distributed in a finely divided state through the second substance called the dispersion medium or dispersing medium. A colloidal substance begins to assume the characteristics of a solution which is indicated by the "infusion" of the substance through membranes. Particles larger than one millimicron

would be categorized as a suspension. It has never been established physiologically that membranes contain pores through which small particles can pass, but the concept of biological transmutation of the elements "in vitro" can quickly explain the phenomena of the colloidal solution's ability to "permeate" cell membranes and establish various balances of ions on opposite surfaces of various membranes within tissues. This concept of biological transmutation explains the rapid transformation of elements in ionic form from one side of the membrane to the other and leads to the understanding of osmotic equilibrium, an important physiological concept.

(16) A chelate comes from the Creek word "chele" which means claw. Therefore, a chelated mineral is a combination of a metal in chemical complexes in which the metal is a part of a ring. In other words, a metallic ion is sequestered and firmly bound into a ring within the chelating molecule. A ring is simply a collection of atoms united in a continuous or closed chain. For example, hemoglobin, the oxygen carrying pigment of the erythrocytes (red blood corpuscle), is a chelate of iron. Chlorophyll, the green coloring matter of plants bu which photosynthesis is accomplished, is a chelate of magnesium. Chelated minerals are considered to be organic in their nature because of complex bonding

with the carbon atom. Chelated minerals are the minerals chemically bound to amino acids wherein chelated minerals are sometimes thought of as a hydrolyzed protein. The chelated minerals activated by enzymes form an alkaline detoxifying agent (chelating agent) which neutralizes the heavy metals and other toxic or foreign substances in the tissues, thus "clawing out" and eliminating them from the body.

It appears from our research that the chelated minerals derived from a plant source, such as the Coenzyme Minerals, are best suited to cleanse and rebuild the body because of their natural ingredients.

It is an established fact that many of the so-called chelated minerals that are made in the laboratory do not have the same effect on the body and must be broken down in the gastrointestinal tract where the form of chelation which is unacceptable in the body is broken down and the free ion is chelated to the degree the body is capable of chelating. Remember, the body can only chelate a small amount of inorganic or non-chelated minerals with the balance having to be removed from the body or else it settles in the tissue of greatest weakness and then shows up as a pigmentation spot in the iris of the eye.

I trust this explains in part the importance of the consumption of chelated minerals in their natural form and why the Coenzyme Minerals are essential to your health in view of the mineral deficient food which is grown today in our chemically poisoned soil.

Please reread the "Twelve Points on Minerals" which is enclosed with this letter.

May this informal letter help put to rest any doubts concerning the effectiveness of this particular universal supplementation. There is so much more that could be said to delve deeper into the whys and wherefores, but let this suffice for now.

Cordially,

John Ray, N.D.

3. **Probiotics-** Prepared Caps available in health food stores. Fermented foods.

As more suppression is accessed you will find it necessary to appropriately increase probiotics. You know you are taking enough when your stool and flatulence no longer has a foul odour indicating a healthy intestinal flora.

1. Lactobacillus bacteria are a group of aerobic, long, slender rods which produce large amounts of lactic acid in the fermentation of carbohydrates.
2. Daily dietary intake of Lactobacillus acidophilus

helps maintain proper balance of healthy bacteria in the intestinal tract. (Some problems from lack of "healthy" bacteria in the intestinal tract due to the proliferation of "unhealthy" bacteria are constipation, irritated colon and diarrhea. Acne, eczema and fever blisters may also be caused by "unhealthy" bacteria.)

3. Lactobacillus acidophilus is essential to help synthesize and assimilate necessary vitamins in the intestinal tract.

4. Lactobacillus acidophilus has been found to help lower cholesterol levels in the blood stream.

5. Lactobacillus acidophilus has been known to help detoxify toxic and hazardous material found in the diet.

6. Lactobacillus acidophilus aids in producing enzymes which help the digestibility of food.

7. Lactobacillus acidophilus improves the digestibility of feed for animals and has been tested and used as a feed additive.

8. Lactobacillus acidophilus helps maintain the pH level of the intestine by producing lactic acid from carbohydrates thus preventing an increase of pH which could then allow the proliferation of sensitive microbes which could produce various toxic substances harmful to the health of the body.

9. Lactobacillus acidophilus helps to replace normal healthy bacteria in the gastro intestinal tract after oral antibiotics have been administered. Oral antimicrobial drugs suppress the drug susceptible components of fecal flora (L. acidophilus) and thus allow, through increased pH, drug resistant strains to become predominant, resulting in loss of benefits derived from normal bacterial activity.

10. There is no known toxicity from ingesting too large a dose of Lactobacillus acidophilus.

11. Lactobacillus acidophilus in the intestinal tract are small in number compared to other organisms. It is, therefore, essential that the human body be assured a maintenance of the proper level of this particular culture by daily ingestion of Lactobacillus acidophilus.

12. Lactobacillus acidophilus is, therefore, justified as a supplemental dietary substance especially in these days when stress, uncertainty and unhealthy pollution of air, water and food predominate. JWR

4. EFA's & DHA-

Organic- Hemp oil, avocado oil, unrefined coconut oil, flax oil (fresh and refrigerated), good quality butter are healthy choices for essential fatty acids. Oils are best assimilated when taken with food.

1. "There are two essential fatty acids. These essentia nutrients have been shown by leading researches to be necessary for both the optimum health of th body as well '~ as far freedom from degenerative disease. They are known as Omega 3 (aipha—linolenic acid or ALNA) and Omega 6 (linoleic acid or LA).

2. Along with proteins, essential fatty acids or EFAs are the building blocks, of cell membranes and various internal cell structures.

3. EFAs are necessary for the metabolism and transportation of triglycerides and cholesterol.

4. EFAs are necessary for the development and the function of the human brain.

5. EFAs are necessary for proper function of vision, the nervous system, adrenal glands, and testes, playing a vital' rolein sperm formation amid conception.

6. EFAs boost metabolism, metabolic rate, energy production, and oxygen uptake.

7. EFAs, particularly Omega 3, have been shown to decrease growth of cancer cells, candida, and various anaerobic organisms destructive to the

health of the body.

8. EFAs are precursors to hormone like substances known as the prostaglandins. There are three main groups of these, known as PG1s, PG2s and PC3s. Prostaglandins govern platelet stickiness in the blood, arterial muscle tone, inflammatory response, sodium excretion through the .kidneys and immune function.

9. PG1s and PG2s are derived from Omega 6, while PG3s come from Omega 3. PG2s are triggered by stress and they will increase platelet stickiness, constrict arteries, increase inflammation, decrease sodium excretion and inhibit immune function. Under normal circumstances the PG3s would keep the PG2s in check; were the production of PG2s to go unchecked serious consequences could well result. A lack or deficiency of Omega 3 will result in a lack or deficiency of PG3s. The ratio of Omega 3 to Omega 6 is also crucial, as excess Omega 6 as compared to Omega 3 promotes tumor formation. Research suggests that the ratio of Omega 6 to Omega 3 should be no greater than 5:1. A typical ratio in most people's diets is in excess of 20:1.

10. Excess non-essential fatty acids compete for a

vital enzyme known as D-6-D, thus an excess of non-essential fatty acids can result in a functional deficiency of EFAs. Research indicates the ratio of non-essential to essential fatty acids should be no more than 1:1. A typical ratio for most people is in excess of 10:1, with almost all of the essential fatty acids being Omega 6.

11. In the November 1986 Journal of the National Cancer Institute research indicated that Omega 3 and one of its derivatives as well as three of the derivatives of Omega 6 were seen to selectively destroy human cancer cells in tissue culture without damaging normal cells.

12. Dr. Johanna Budwig, a German M.D. and biochemist, discovered that the blood of cancer patients was deficient in EFAs. A yellow-green pigment was found in place of the normal red blood pigment or hemoglobin. Along with certain dietary improvements, she gave her patients three tablespoons of fresh flax oil as a means of getting EFAs into the body (flax oil is 55-65Z Omega 3 and 15-25Z Omega 6). On this program, which in~1uded no other supplements, she found that within three months the yellow-green was replaced by red and cancer disappeared."
Douglas Morrison

5. Magnesium- (2 part mag-1 part calcium)
Assists in the breaking up the melanin protein that may act as a barrier in the monopoles- see HWH.

6. Raw Protein/ Amino Acids
Eating raw food that has not been denatured by cooking, processing, pasteurization, etc., contains the natural enzymes necessary for digestion. Eat prior to cooked food for optimum digestion. Raw bee pollen (assimilated best by crushing and taken with a little honey) and lentil/bean sprouts are good sources of raw protein.
 Our body requires 20 amino acids in its raw form in order that all bodily metabolic functions can operate properly- so endocrine glands can produce and secrete all the necessary hormones for complete cellular functions. If there is one amino acid missing in the diet due to cooking the food we consume, or due to eating processed foods, or due to the inability of the body to digest protein, or eating a protein deficient diet, then certain hormones cannot be produced and secreted by the endocrine glands. Two of the 9 essential amino acids, tryptophan and lysine, are destroyed by heating/cooking at approx. 107 degrees F

7. Aerobic Oxygen- follow directions on label.

This concludes the basic nutritional program for the practice of Body Electronics. After following this program for 20 plus years, and knowing hundreds of other that have even longer experience, it is clear to me the genius of the essential combination of nutrients tha may provide what is required for hormone regeneration rebooting our endocrine system, supplies necessary nutrients we no longer get in our diet, and effectively allows for the activation of the electric body.
This is necessary to precede the activity of consciousness change within the parameters of Body Electronics.

Writing on Mercury Toxicity by John Whitman Ray

1. I have had the pleasure of testing several hundred patients and students in my field of Body Electronics with the Jerome Mercury Vapor Analyzer. I have found only two people in all my testing who have not evidenced a continual toxic exposure to mercury vapor emanating from silver amalgam dental fillings under normal chewing compression.
2. Dentists have been educated to believe that once

mercury has been combined into the filling material, it remains "locked in" and can't come out. The sad fact is that there is absolutely no scientific research in existence to support this hypothesis. To the contrary, all evidence indicates that silver amalgam containing approximately 50% mercury is a source of extreme toxic elemental mercury adversely affecting the health of the human body.

3. Evidence now demonstrates that surface particles of the amalgam filling material are being chemically broken down and released into the o~al cavity. These minute particles of mercury filling are acted upon by oral and intestinal bacteria to produce methyl mercury, an even more toxic form of mercury than elemental mercury with target areas being primarily the pituitary gland, thyroid gland and the brain.

4. It has been demonstrated that dissimilar metals in the mouth can also contribute to electrical activity and corrosion (much like a battery) and can result in unexplained pain, ulcerations, inflammation and disruption of corresponding meridians in the body.

5. The presence of mercury in dental amalgam fillings has been shown conclusively to adversely affect the body's immune response. It has been

shown that after amalgam removal the red and white blood cell levels tend to seek normal range with a corresponding increase in the body's immune response as evidenced by T-lymphocyte count increase.

6. Research has indicated that mercury is the single most toxic metal that has been investigated, even more toxic than lead, cadmium or arsenic.

7. The International Conference on Biocompatibility of Materials was held in November 1988 in Colorado Springs, Colorado, U.S.A. Many of the world authorities on mercury and mercury toxicity met to discuss the issue of dental amalgam and other materials used in dentistry. Their official conclusion was drafted and signed which read: "Based on the known toxic potential of mercury and its documented release from dental amalgams, usage of mercury containing amalgam increases the health risk of the patients, the dentists and dental personnel."

8. Autopsy studies from Sweden and Germany show a positive statistical correlation between the number of occiusal surfaces of dental amalgam and mercury levels in the brain and kidney cortex. It would be wise to point out that both elemental mercury and organic methyl mercury were found in brain tissue

upon autopsy.

9. Dr. David Eggleston of the University of California, found a T-lymphocyte count of 47% (ideal levels are between 70-80%) in patients with silver amalgam fillings. After removal of the amalgams the T-lymphocyte count rose to 73%.

10. Multiple sclerosis patients have been found to have 8 times higher levels of mercury in the cerebrospinal fluid compared to neurologically healthy controls. Inorganic mercury is capable of producing symptoms which are indistinguishable from those of multiple sclerosis.

11. It is the responsibility of every dentist and doctor to inform and educate their patients to the effect that:

a) Mercury is contained in most dental filling material and all silver amalgam material.

b) Mercury in fillings can have toxic effects on some persons. Manifestations of the disease of mercury poisoning starts to become apparent three to ten years after the insertion of the mercury.

c) There are alternative materials that could be used on dental fillings that could have after effects on the individual.

d) The patient has the right to insist that an alternative material be used.

e) The freedom of individual choice in health care shall be inherently respected and preserved as an individual right and responsibility of free men everywhere.

12. One must remember that the diagnosis of mercury intoxication is extremely difficult to ascertain because of the insidious nature of the onset of symptoms and because of most physicians unfamiliarity or misinformation concerning proper testing techniques. Unfortunately, mercury is so-toxic to the human organism, that there can be cell death or irreversible chemical damage long before clinical observable symptoms appear indicating that something is wrong. Since organic mercury in some body tissues (e.g. brain) has a half life of over 25 years (i.e. it takes the body 25 years to get rid of ~ of a single dose of mercury under normal circumstances) it is only a matter of time and degree of exposure until some form of symptomology appears. With all this in mind we cannot fool with mercury toxicity or delay the "safe" removal of silver amalgam fillings by the hands of a knowledgeable and responsible dentist.

Water-Hydration

It is essential to drink sufficient amounts of quality spring water. Take care to compensate for the dehydrating effects of heat, caffeine, alcohol, exercise, etc.

During the practice of Body Electronics and the detoxing effects of the nutritional program one must remain vigilant to stay hydrated each and every day.

One half the body's weight in ounces per day is minimal hydration.

150 lbs. body weight= 75 oz. water per day

Read- The Bodies Many Cries for Water
by F. Batmanghelidj MD

Be Still and Breathe

These are the second and third physical principles afte
nutrition. The practice of being still, while breathing
deep and regular prepares the physical body for
Pointholding. Mastering physical principles allows for
the opening of the emotional body. Begin with fifteen
minutes and increase to one hour per day.

The classic three part breath:

Spine straight.

Inhale deep into the lower abdomen, mid-sternum to
the clavicle. Exhale first from the clavicle area, to the
mid-sternum, and finally the abdomen, pulling in the
abdomen to release all the air. Like filling a glass then
pouring it out.

Do so without pausing, keeping the
inhalation/exhalation equal in duration.

Be aware of the breath, while holding perfectly still,
(allow the abdomen to move with the breath)
remembering to not allow the breath to pause at any
time.

Many other physical considerations such as exercise,
dental- mercury amalgam toxicity and root canals,
fluoride, sleep, vaccinations, electromagnetic
pollution....etc. may be found in How We Heal.

➢ How We Heal, Doug Morrison
www.howweheal.com

Logic In Sequence Series
➢ Book One- The Laws of
Perfection
➢ Book Two- Health and the
Human Mind, The Healing
Crisis
➢ Book Three- Health and the
Human Mind
➢ The Electrification of Matter
by Dr. John Whitman Ray
➢ Locating and Holding Points in Body Electronics
by Peter Hinde
www.bodyelectronics.co.uk

➢ The Body Electric- Electromagnetism and the
Foundation of Life
by Robert O. Becker, M.D. and Gary Selden

➢ The Science and Practice of Iridology Vol I and II
by Bernard Jensen, D.C, Ph.D.
➢ Grey's Anatomy- the study of the anatomy and
physiology of the human body.

The Healing Crisis

➢ Read again and again, The Law of Healing Crisis by JWR, in the Twelve Points on Body Electronics.

We all must be active participants in the unfolding of our own potentialities. The doorway through which all must pass is always open. You choose to become different than you are now when you decide to take personal responsibility. The path has infinite patience, the Path of Freedom.

We have created our present circumstances from the top down. This is to say we stepped into the four bodies sequentially; spiritual, mental, emotional and physical. Now in the process of Body Electronics we go back the way we came in reverse order.

A simplification of the Healing Crisis: It may feel worse before it feels better. Hyperactivity precedes relative level of balance.

In the first few years of embracing the Healing Crisis, I began to see many aspects of myself I was previously unaware of. As awareness increased I became much more aware of resistance patterns I was previously unwilling to see, and so it goes.

The physical, emotional and mental aspects that come forth to be released are what we are capable of, yet at times this may feel overwhelming. We all have spiritual help, ask and receive in gratitude.

"In the physical body it has been discovered in every cell a nearly indestructible material which is composed of a melanin-protein complex. This is an organic computer chip full of stored memory, which acts in a stimulus- response manner. *This organic computer chip determines the reaction, which is stimulated by an environmental activity.* This "crystal" or stimulus- response structure is like a filtered prism, which allows only that information to pass which is programmed to pass. The receptors may be fully activated to receive environmental stimuli but the information received is programmed into reactive patterns of which the individual may or may not be aware. At best the individual is aware of the reaction but may not be aware of the stimulus that causes the reaction. Nearly all that is received at the level of the filtered prism or melanin protein complex is blocked and converted to a response pre-programmed to respond to a specific stimulus. *This stimulus-response conditioned mechanism inherent within the crystal below the awareness of the individual, being' the end result of suppressed or resisted experiences.*

Only a small amount of the entire electromagnetic spectrum or energy field is allowed to penetrate or gain entry to our awareness through a limited window in the organic computer chip until we individually become capable of gradually expanding the opening or window to allow more "light" to penetrate without being blocked or converted into a response which is automatic. This additional light or understanding can only come with experience. We cannot perceive something, which we are incapable of experiencing on the mental level. We cannot remember that which is in a constant state of suppression through a continuation of a state of resistance. That which is consciously suppressed or is below the level of consciousness is physiologically manifested as a stimulus-response conditioned reflex. We cannot visualize that which we have suppressed. Remember, from Chapter Three in Book One of the Logic in Sequence Series, it has been clearly indicated that *pain a the capstone to memory and not until we have re-experienced on the mental level the emotional and/or physical pain, concerning a specified event, will we ever be able to have the clear ability to visualize that particular event.* Resistance to a given specific event and visualization of the same event are incompatible, therefore *we cannot fully visualize until all resistance is overcome.* All in all, we perceive only that which we have not denied or resisted, as determined by our unique hologram of thought, feeling and spoken word, as determined by our unique manner of resistance.

UNTIL MANKIND CAN EXPERIENCE ON THE MENTAL LEVEL THAT WHICH EXISTS ON THE PHYSICAL LEVEL, HE WILL BE BOUND TO THE PHYSICAL." JWR

Some Basic Principles-

Commitment- Logic In Sequence- Book 1 pg. 91-98

"Without commitment, there would be no action, as action is a determination to apply a law with faith. This is a commitment." J.W.R.

Prayer- Logic In Sequence-Book 1 pg. 187-195
As we continue on the upscale movement through the emotional body, we observe/experience the constant changes in regards to prayer.
Gratitude- How We Heal, pg. 60-61

Thankfulness that is so powerful tears cannot be stopped.

Faith- How We Heal, pg. 61-62
 See- Ten steps to Perfection

Love- How We Heal, pg. 57-59
 The feeling/energy of Love is what we access to transmute resistance.
 The Love that exists within us, ALWAYS...we uncover this Power of Powers continuously.
This is what attracted me to practice and continue in Body Electronics.
The growing awareness of Love.

Grace-
Ask for guidance and receive.

Morphogenetic Resonance
HWH-pg. 30-33
 In B.E. we witness change in others as a result of change in ourselves. Some of this can be attributed to attitude (our change), yet some changes can only be explained by morphogenetic resonance. This commonly occurs within family members (DNA pattern), yet is not limited to this. In comparison to the tuning fork that

vibrates out and whatever is in resonance, will begin to vibrate also. So it is with the vibration of regeneration.

Humour- while facilitating pointholding~

Knowing when (or not) to apply humor, is very important with the practice of B.E., let the Spirit move you. I have spent years receiving teachings with Ojibwe people and have been shown over the years how humor is applied at just the right moment to 'lighten up' a very serious moment (teaching).

As with everything, done in the spirit of nonresistance is the key. Do not become intellectually involved in the pointholdee's story while pointholding.

Maintain impartiality to the best of your ability.

Humility-

See- Ten steps to Perfection

Humility is increasingly experienced as one moves upscale to greater levels of awareness. The gradual realization of Oneness as it is experienced.

Discernment- we know from the present perspective, as with all things, this is constantly changing as we move upscale.

Self-Honesty- required in increasing amounts as one moves upscale, courageously looking deeper.

'The List'

The list assists us in organizing our lives amidst the constant rearrangement the Universe makes within the Healing Crisis.

Taken from LIS-Book One, JWR

"Put down on a list all your goals.
Put down on the same list all your desires. Make sure you weigh carefully whether these goals and desires are to resolve Karma and thus are evolutionary in nature through the process of Karmic transmutation, or are the goals and desires going to create more Karma and thus bring the individual, first person included, down the dwindling involutionary spiral into identification with matter through the continuation of resistance.
Put down on the list all your responsibilities. Make sure that these responsibilities are what you sincerely believe are your responsibilities that are for your own individual growth and development, or are these responsibilities those that others have put on you? Each person must be true to his own heart in regards to these matters. It is good to be aware of other's

ideas but the final decision regarding the direction of our life is our own and we alone must bear the burden of that decision. Put down on the same list alt those uncompleted acts such as repayment of debts, fixing the broken tools, repairing the window, tacking down the carpet, waxing the car, sewing on the button, finishing the book, etc. This part of the list becomes rather extensive at times because we have left many things undone. These need our attention, in proper time and place. Now, let us be honest with ourselves. On the list we must put those areas, which need making amends. Where have we done a person wrong where we need to make satisfactory restitution that harmony may again prevail? This is a tall order because here we deal often times with justification of our actions, emotions that are out of control, decisions to never speak again, never trust again, never do this again, never do that again. These areas of concern need to be weighed and determined as to how or what can we do to bring harmony into areas of disharmony. Of course, it takes two to resolve matters between two people, but it is better to have things resolved, if possible, rather than leave a condition hanging. It is better to know that we have done all that is within our power to resolve conflicts so that a certain degree of peace prevails if it only exists in our own mind. Put all these areas of confusion and disorder among personal relationships on the list with the resolve to make things right, to the very best of our ability. There will be various and sundry items that we will put on our list for whatever reason. We don't have to manufacture a reason. We have decided and that is reason enough. We are responsible to put order in our life, that is our sole responsibility. The great German philosopher Goethe stated "Great things are done in secret". This is such a true statement. Do not show your list to another. If you and your mate have a list, that is between the two of you.

But for your own list, keep it between you and your God presence, that responsibility of decision may be learned. Now, let us organize the list. Put all your items on one list so they can be weighed and pondered together. Time factors need to be considered. Prior commitments must be taken into consideration. Priorities have to be weighed in the balance. Opportunities provided by time and chance may require prompt action. Place the difficult things to accomplish at the top of the list, place the simple things at the bottom of the list and begin with the simplest. At this time it would be wise to again read the poem.

TO SEARCH FOR THINGS BEYOND OUR GRASP IS
FANTASY,
WHEN THAT WHICH LIES WITHIN OUR REACH WE SEE
HAS NOT YET BEEN COMPLETED, YET HOLDS THE
KEY,
TO THAT WHICH THROUGH RIGHT ACTION OURS WILL
BE.
THE SIMPLEST THINGS IN LIFE WILL MAKE US FREE.

Start at the bottom of the list. Everything eventually will have to be done. So wouldn't it be wise to do everything from a position of success where we can see the end from the beginning in every act? This is a virtue of the Gods as in the creation of the earth, every single act could be seen completed from the mental level before it occurred on the physical. Then it was stated "It is good." In like manner, we plan out the simplest item in our mind from beginning to end - we can see the end from the beginning. Then we act and make sure it is finished just like we had decided it was to be. Tell no one what you are going to do unless it concerns them, as people have a tendency to always have an opinion as to whether it was done right or wrong which is a judgement. Be willing to take the flak of judgement for when you make your own decisions you are now in the arena and must be willing to subject yourself to the opinions of others.

Stand your ground and say I did it the way I decided to do it and it is good. It is reasonable to gather as much information as possible about any given task or project - this is simply good sense. Yet, when all the information is in, the decision for action is in your hands. *Make your decision, act upon it, and be willing to take the consequences of that action.* This type of procedure increases the ability to take responsibility and to think for oneself. If you do not think for yourself, you will find many other people from all walks of life very willing to do your thinking for you. On your individual list do your own thinking and learn to be a person of responsibility - we discussed this in earlier chapters. If you are dealing with another person such as a mate or business partner then come to common consent on a common list and share your thinking and come to terms and corresponding action. If dealing with a group, work within the lowest common denominator of mutual acceptance or agreement. Do not talk over your private business with another unless it concerns that person. Your business between your mate and yourself should be kept confidential between the two of you. The same principle applies to a group or corporation. Keep the order of business within the group. *In any case when your business is known outside of those who need to know, it has a tendency to weaken the resolve.* As we progress from the simplest item on the list and complete that, we move on to the next simplest item on our list and then complete that. It is obvious to the candid and reflective mind that if we fill our life with successful experience it is reasonable to see that the items at the top of the list will eventually secure a position at or near the bottom, eventually to be mastered. I have had the pleasure of teaching this simplicity to hundreds of thousands over about 30 years and many have used the "List" with wonderful results. Please consider the following concept. Much of what has not been mastered on our list is simply our own Karma, which is the summation of our resistances. Each item on the list has in some way drawn our attention and therefore has manifested in our environment in some unique way for us to deal with.' JWR

The Laws of Love Light and Perfection

The Clean Heart- The Holy Science- Sutra 30
'Through true repentance (forgiveness/love) man
reaches Maharloka (the 'great world'). No longer

subject to the influence of
ignorance, he attains a
clean heart. He enters the
NATURAL caste of the
Brahmanas ("knowers of
Brahma"). Then man
becomes able to
comprehend the Spiritual
Light, Brahma, the Real
Substance in the universe.
Not merely reflecting but
manifesting Spiritual Light,
man rises to the kingdom
of God. Abandoning the
vain idea of his separate
existence, he enters
Satyaloka, wherein he attains the state of final release o
Kaivalya, oneness with Spirit.

-Sri Yukteswa

Applying the Law of Love
that includes Forgiveness and Gratitude
Transmutation of the Emotional Body with
The Three Powers

In the presence of enthusiasm (lovingly and willingly enduring all things), the 'crystals' in the human body begin to dissolve, yielding up suppressed thoughts, feelings (emotionality) and words (word patterns present in the crystal). At this time we are given opportunity to actively participate in transmuting patterns with the Power of Unconditional Love and Unconditional Forgiveness.

This requires the focus of intensifying what is unfolding and maintaining all three creative aspects simultaneously.

Memory -Emotion –Words
Be in the sensory memory, in other words bring it into the PRESENT. Feel what is there, say the words (internally or externally) and encompass it ALL with Love and Forgiveness. It is simple yet not always easy. When the emotional body experiences transmutation, pathways are opened and upscale (evolutionary) movement occurs.

This is the upscale movement of the seven times seven, in the emotional body model we use in B.E.

Coldness in and around the body is what can be explained in terms of atomic endothermic reaction. (see How We Heal, 363-64) Simplistically, the body is using energy (drawing it in) to change it into something else. (biological transmutation)

The atomic exothermic reaction is experienced as heat in and around the body. The body is releasing the energy. This can be described as simplicity moving into complexity. You may study this further in Book Three LIS. This increases in intensity (awareness) as one moves upscale through the seven times seven levels of emotionality. I have experienced simultaneous endothermic/exothermic reactions several times, freezing cold and burning up at the same time. In retrospect, I see that these experiences predicated major consciousness change.

The Hereditary Level
Genetics- DNA Imprints

Our soul through vibration is attracted to the genetic structure of the parents with which we come into physical being. We often find the same, a small amount of the same or the opposite of the resistance pattern(s) in our ancestors and children. We also can 'remember' a relative's memory. Take what we get and work with it. Transmutation of a genetic pattern creates a ripple effect through our connected ancestry, through morphogenetic resonance, regardless of where they are at present, in physical form or not.

The Soul Level

We each have created a unique soul history. It is our stored patterns of resistance, often accompanied by trauma we are looking for, in order for it to be released. The patterns we are looking for exist in this life, although it is common to 'find' ourselves in past life (or occasional future) situations requiring release. Take what you find and work with it.

The Entity Level

'It should be clearly understood that an entity is not the cause of any of our resistances, but more of an effect. A particular resistance will create a hole in our energy /auric field.' HWH pg. 29

These self-created 'holes' will sometimes fill with separate intelligence, but mostly it is our own repeated programming that we judge as separate intelligence.

With love and respect, we offer it ALL to the great recycler, when we transmute the pattern. I recall a pointholding session, when I released hundreds of animal entities I had attracted through sympathy/attachment. They were all so willing and happy to move on.

Commanding with Love~ How We Heal pg. 26-30
LIS Book Book Two pg. 77-105

Trust- See LIS Book One-pg.131
True Trust (being in the moment without resistance) is a quality of perfection. Letting it happen/Making it happen simultaneously. Trust is viewed/experienced differently as one moves up the scale of emotion.

Transmutation of the Mental Body
Applying the Laws of Light

When transmutation (embracing-intensifying-forgiving-loving, changing consciousness) occurs within the emotional body, we gradually gain access to the mental body. At the emotional level of pain we begin to see duality along with our judgement (to both sides). The level of pain (and access to the mental body) is in direct relation to where on the 7X7 we are. At this point we may access the Violet Flame (an electric/pranic force within), making it possible to transmute the mental body. First we encompass the viewed duality (see both sides), become aware of the 'violet flame', and direct its power for the purpose of transmutation. Beyond the Violet Flame of Transmutation is the Three Fold Flame, light vibrations of Love (pink), Light (gold) and Perfection of Power (blue). This Heart Flame resonates from the Source within us all- It is within all life- accessing/ being in harmony with this light requires the emotional body and corresponding nervous system (cerebral spinal flow) to be open and cleared. This is the Work. The Universal 'fail safe'- we cannot access this level until much of the emotional body has been actively transmuted. Higher consciousness is realized from the bottom (physical) up, encompassing ALL in love (energy of) within the emotional body, eventually accessing greater levels of the mental body where one may choose to encompass the self- created patterns of resistance that then lead to the spiritual components of life.

Observe, Receive, Recreate and Release.
➢ READ- LIS-Book Three, pg. 928

Encompassment of Duality is applied (holding both sides with focused concentration), while accessing and directing the Violet Flame, until equanimity is experienced. The duality being observed will gradually become ONE/In Harmony once again when fully transmuted.

➢ READ- LIS-Book Three, pg. 532

DO NOT LET THE FOCUS ON THE OUTER INTERFERE WITH CONTINUAL INNER INTROSPECTION AND APPROPRIATE CHANGE IN CONSCIOUSNESS. JWR~

Zero Ohms Resistance
& the Time/Space Continuum Warp

'To experience the Time-Space-Continuum-Warp one must be capable of being cause and being effect simultaneously while re-creating the resistance to being both cause and effect and re-creating the resistance to the resistance of being both cause and effect' JWR
  ➤LIS Book 3, pg 956

'One encompasses darkness by focusing on the light. One encompasses death by focusing on life. One cannot learn about the light by focusing on darkness. The light comprehends darkness, but darkness does not comprehend light. Life comprehends death but death does not comprehend life. One cannot comprehend love by focusing on resistance, but by focusing on love the love encompasses, comprehends and dispels the resistance.' JWR
I include this advanced material so we have knowledge of the vastness of Body Electronics. These topics and advanced disciplines are taught and practiced in the Visualization and Consciousness course.

We begin from the bottom up, applying (obeying) physical laws then emotional laws, mental laws, and spiritual law, until ALL flows in Harmony.
ONE LEARNS TO EXPERIENCE THE YIN ASPECT OF LIFE WITH MENTAL NON-RESISTANCE (Love), WHILE, SIMULTANEOUSLY, ONE LEARNS TO EXPERIENCE THE YANG ASPECT OF LIFE WITH MENTAL NON-RESISTANCE JWR~

Applying the Law of Perfection

Ten Steps to Perfection
Book 1- Logic In Sequence- JWR

STEP ONE: Faith.

The first step is faith, which has been described to you as *"the assurance of things hoped for, the evidence of things not* seen. "This could be expressed another way:
"through the acquisition of knowledge one foresees as having already happened the everpresent now".
One must have an increasing depth of perceptive awareness in the now to understand the deepening aspects of faith. It requires an act of faith to acknowledge the yin energies of life as the end result

of the creative aspects of man.

Responsibility is claiming the perceptual nowness as one's own creation, which is only the first step of responsibility.

STEP TWO: Virtue.

The second step to perfection is to appropriately apply the laws of God, carefully moving from the appropriate application of the lower laws to higher laws.

Responsibility is the obtaining of the law and then coming to the understanding of the law by maintaining the law through application.

The application of law through faith is known as virtue. Virtue is faithfully being obedient to the law from which one derives knowledge.

STEP THREE: Knowledge

The third step to perfection is to come to the understanding of the law through application, which results in knowledge.

Knowledge can only come from experience.

Knowledge cannot be bought as an intellectual curiosity in the market place but must be earned

through the assiduous application of law.
Knowledge can only be obtained through faithful compliance with the law.

STEP FOUR: Temperance.

The fourth step to perfection is
understanding that there are higher and lower laws
and understanding when to apply them to oneself and
to others. This is known as temperance. Wisdom
dictates when one obeys a lower law or a higher law.
*Whenever a higher law is obeyed it necessitates
breaking a lower law with the corresponding penalty
for breaking a lower law. A lower law should never be
broken unless it is "covered" by obedience to a
higher law.*
Temperance, then, is wisdom self-applied to a given
condition demanding attention resulting in choices or
alternatives of solution.

STEP FIVE: Patience.

The fifth step is patience. Here is where one lovingly
and willingly allows the joyous antics of a free soul to
move toward, ultimate perfection according to the
dictates of his own conscious and at this own rate of

speed. Each pathway is planned to be traveled according to the unique rhythm of that individual traveler.

The free agency of the soul is to be honored and respected and never denied as long as the actions do not interfere with the free agency of another.

STEP SIX: Brotherly/ Sisterly Kindness:

The sixth step is brotherly kindness, which simply is the exercise of the Golden Rule. "Do unto others as you would have them do unto you." This is true as long as we can place ourselves fully into the viewpoint and understanding of the other with his/her expectations and conditions, and his/her level of awareness of enduring ability to the experiences of life.

STEP SEVEN: Godliness.

The seventh step is Godliness, the ability to administer the law as a mother and a father would administer the law to his or her own children. *In this arena of responsibility all is designed for the gradual release of the soul from restriction as one*

helps the other to help himself.
One disciplines lovingly until that individual can discipline oneself. One helps the individual become more proficient at the choice of his own interest, directing that interest until it encompasses every phase of life's activity without resistance.

STEP EIGHT: Charity.

The eighth step to perfection is charity, the pure love of the inner Christlight, continually manifested through every outer act with no conditions or expectations. Only love is manifested, ever sustained and ever outflowing, with no judgement, as love can only come from non-resistance and discernment.

STEP NINE: Humility.

The ninth step is humility. One is humble when there is no longer separation but a recognition from a multidimensional point of view and a multiple viewpoint of consideration that all is one. That all is one continuous, uninterrupted cause of life which is simultaneously cause and effect and there are no mistakes. *All is perfect divine order.*
This is the beginning of understanding the true

position of "Unity in Diversity".
STEP TEN: Diligence.

The tenth step to perfection is obtained after each of the prior steps toward perfection. The tenth step is diligence. One cannot be truly diligent, therefore one cannot be truly responsible until all steps are mastered in sequence, indicating mastery of our linear thinking capacity and then, finally, as a mastery of our hologramic oneness encompassing the appropriate simultaneous yin/ yang activity in each event of life as it is served up sequentially as the condition demands. Responsibility, therefore, is the qualities of perfection appropriately applied in our lives, individually and collectively,   as we love, communicate, and create while we dance the dance of life. The Law of Right Action leads one step by step to perfection and the full application of responsibility. One must first of all receive before one can give. One must first of all serve apprenticeship before one can be released to be a master. One must first of all be willing to be the effect before he/she can become cause, then simultaneously cause and effect.

~Yin/Yang~
The Torroidal Electromagnetic Field

One was first cause, then one's creation was resisted thus crystallizing this creation in the universe to form a continuous outer (yin) manifestation of the that which was resisted (and is being resisted constantly in the eve present now). Then one resisted the outer manifestation (resisted the resistance) and further crystallized oneself. Now, all this must be undone in reverse order. We first of all must be willing to be the effect of the "yin" manifestations around us (non-resist the resistance). This entails the perfect development of the application of the concept of non-resistance. Once one is willing to be the effect and can encompass the concept of resistance - non-resistance in reference to any given outer event, then we are capable of dealing with the cause. We must then be willing to be cause and encompass the resistance we once had to being cause where we denied our part in the creative process. This entails responsibility which includes lovingly and willingly enduring all things", which includes embracing our causal relationship to life with resistance - non-resistance. This is not an intellectual exercise but an experiential adventure, wherein one plunges oneself into the dance of life with enthusiasm and non-resistance with the understanding that one must re-experience the resistance to being "cause" before he can come to the point of non-resistance to the specified function of a specific creative act, (yang), and thus view the inner essence, the source of all creativity.

Some Contraindications for practicing Body Electronics

Pregnancy- Pointholding is to be postponed during pregnancy and breastfeeding.

Varicose veins- do not apply any amount of pressure or massage on or near varicosities.

I.U.D.s- Intra-uterine device- pelvic points, bladder lift, spinal points etc. are not to be held when IUD is present.

Psychiatric Patients- a person who has taken drugs to suppress symptoms of mental imbalance must be fully aware of the level of self- responsibility and commitment required before ever embarking upon undoing the suppressed condition. All others involved with the person including doctors, must be fully informed and in agreement to proceed.

Organ Transplants and Medical Implants- People who have undergone these medical interventions and/or on immunosuppressive drugs, are not to practice B.E. The organ/artificial part could be rejected when the H.C. occurs and the immune system is stimulated. Although this has not occurred, we must remember to first do no harm.

Tumors- never apply pressure on or near a tumor.

Osteoporosis- Paralysis or numbness- extreme care when applying pressure, as the pointholdee cannot tell you when it is too much.

This applies to spinal cord injuries, diabetic nerve damage or any condition where circulation is impaired.

Pinch test general nerve sensitivity by comparing the sensation from the inner soft tissue under your arm at the armpit, pinching down the inner arm to the end of your third finger.

Soft Abdominal Cavity- Due to many contraindications that may be present here, we do not hold anywhere on soft tissue in the abdomen. Nor do we hold near the abdominal aorta.

> See- Locating and Holding Points in Body Electronics,

by Peter Hinde www.bodyelectronics.co.uk   pg.91

Cranial points- no cranial points are held until Cranial Electronics.

> See How We Heal pg. 276-280

> Consult your medical professionals.

Addiction-Habits-Self Medication

The unconscious program to not feel stimulates the compulsion to self-medicate with food, caffeine, sugar, tobacco, alcohol, recreational drugs, exercise, etc.

Fasting from sugars, caffeine, and other suppressive substance/activity before during and after a Pointholding event is necessary.

"Self-medication involves the suppression of discomfor by moving ourselves down to a lower level of balance and comfort. In regards to both sugar and alcohol, two of the most common forms of self-medication, is highly influenced by the individual's nutritional status." How We Heal pg. 414

As we move our nutrition upscale, we experience less and less desire to self-medicate. This takes continuous efforts and perseverance.

Habitual use of recreational drugs that includes alcoh and tobacco must be discontinued well prior to participating in Body Electronics Intensives held by me.

The Emotional Body

Moving upscale through the emotional body allows for increasing awareness of Unconditional Love and Unconditional Forgiveness. Start with what you can access and expand from there. Awareness gradually increases as we re-experience and release from unconsciousness to enthusiasm (7X7). See diagram on page 354-355 LIS-Book Two. It shows how the forty nine levels of emotion create the wave length (vibration), the Yang/cause -Yin/effect.

Endocrine Reflex- Emotionality-Focused Expression

Level One-Pineal-Enthusiasm-Creativity- Love

Level Two- Pituitary- Pain- Intuition

Level Three- Thyroid- Anger- Power/Control ~
                                    (Specific Memory)

Level Four- Heart/Thymus- Fear- Security

Level Five- Pancreas/Adrenals- Grief- Victimization
                                    (General Memory)

Level Six- Spleen- Apathy-
Involvement without responsibility

Level Seven- Gonads- Unconsciousness- Sex and
reproduction

Seven Levels within Seven Levels- 7X7

Read- The Mystery of the Seven Times Seven
Explained- Chapter 13- LIS Book Two pg. 3
Suppression-Venting-Control

Suppression is held in the
physical/emotional/mental/spiritual unconscious.
In B.E. we are asking for this to be revealed. As it is
observed enthusiastically, we begin to feel more of
what's there.Venting is a necessary part of the
transmutation process. Venting is in no way
projection upon anyone or anything. When one feels
perfectly willing to vent and has done so, the attempt
to control the emoting while still feeling the emotion
within is the next step. Following sufficient venting
(intensified) we then move to control (contain) the
emotion within. Holding the emotion intensely
without emoting, the feeling of the emotion will

increase. If this occurs and we enthusiastically contain within, encompassing in unconditional love, then we experience a thorough transmutation and rapid upscale movement. If there isn't an increase of intensity of the present emotion when we contain (control) then we go back to venting, until we feel ready to contain again. This takes a lot of effort. Venting is a necessary part of the transmutation process. When thorough release (applying the laws of Love/Light) of the held memory/emotion and words has been experienced, only then we attempt to control the emotion. Holding the emotion without emoting, the feeling (awareness) of the emotion increases.
By control, we move upscale.
If there isn't an increase of intensity of the present emotion when we contain (control) then we go back to venting.

Pointholding-
Applying Sustained Acupressure-

In holding points we discover increasingly greater ability to give as well as to receive. The pointholding process requires study and experience.

It is not a mechanical process, in other words
Pointholding is an increasingly intuitive process within
a framework of application.
Pointholding is sequential as seen on the flow sheet.
Accompanied by a certified B.E. Instructor.

BODY ELECTRONICS
FLOW SHEET

1_____ STO	20_____Large Intestine
plus_____Pancreas	21_____Eyes
_____Heart	22_____Ears
_____Heart Firing	23_____Spine--Atlas--1st Cervical
_____Other	24_____Spine--Axis--2nd Cervical
2_____Pineal	25_____Spine--Cervicals
3_____Hypothalamus	26_____Spine--Thoracic
4_____Pituitary	27_____Spine--Lumbar
5_____Medulla	28_____Spine--Sacrum
6_____Thyroid/Parathyroid	29_____Spine--Coccyx
7_____Thymus	30_____Spine--Curvature
8_____Heart-Bronchials-Lungs	31_____Anterior Cervicals
9_____Heart firing mechanism	32_____Triple Axis Clavicle
10_____Solar Plexus	33_____Pubic Bone
11_____Pancreas	34_____Ischial Tuberosity
12_____Adrenals-Kidneys	35_____Sternum
13_____Spleen	36_____Cranial
14_____Liver-Gall Bladder	37_____Bladder Lift
15_____Gonads-Ovaries-Testes	38_____Hiatus Hernia
16_____Prostate-Uterus	39_____Other
17_____Bladder	40_____Other
18_____Stomach	41_____Other
19_____Small Intestine	42_____Other

Once this basic sequence has been completed, one is well advised to return to earlier stages, where greater and deeper results can then be attained.
Electric Shock N.D.E. Heart Attack Stroke Cancer Coma Tie-Ins:

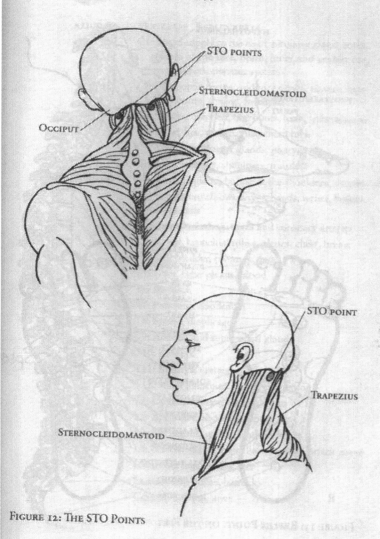

Figure 12: The STO Points

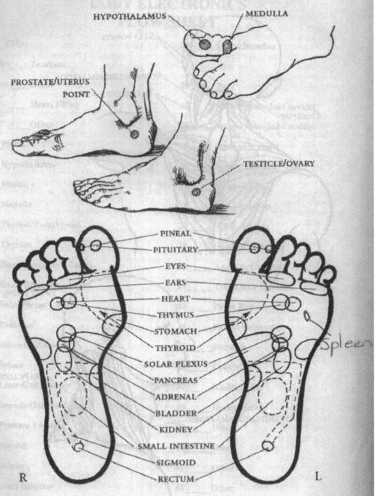

fig13.jpg

HYPOTHALAMUS   MEDULLA

PROSTATE/UTERUS
POINT

TESTICLE/OVARY

PINEAL
PITUITARY
EYES
EARS
HEART
THYMUS
STOMACH
THYROID
SOLAR PLEXUS
PANCREAS
ADRENAL
BLADDER
KIDNEY
SMALL INTESTINE
SIGMOID
RECTUM

Spleen

R   L

FIGURE 13: REFLEX POINTS ON THE FEET

106

Locating and Holding Points

One must be taught correct location and application by a Certified Body Electronics Instructor.

Holding the STO points- see diagram, pg. 58
Find the 'valley between the Sternocleidomastoid and Trapezius muscles, follow it upward toward the occiput (bone at base of cranium) fall back off of the occiput slightly and apply correct directional pressure.
Directional pressure- in toward the spine (medial), up toward the ceiling (anterior), and back toward the top of the head (superior). With concentrated effort see the pressure directed to the centre of the forehead.
STO's reflex to circulation and nerve supply.
They are the first points on the flow sheet for this reason,
typically held with the middle fingers.
There is often a great deal of numbness with this point.
As a pointholder be aware of the positioning at all times. Do not allow the fingers to slide toward the ear, use the vision, if fingers/hands become numb.

Pointholding gradually increases focus and concentration, be patient with yourself as you move upscale, both as a pointholder and pointhldee.

➤ Peter Hinde's book, Locating and Holding Points in Body Electronics is a must have for pointholding groups. www.bodyelectronics.co.uk

"One must remember that the crystals are encoded thought patterns, word patterns and emotions that are held by the crystal in a state of continual creation twenty-four hours a day. Changing our thinking is not enough. Making affirmations is not enough. We have to undo that which has already been created. We have to dissolve the crystal through application of the appropriate laws and then become aware of the though patterns, word patterns and emotionality. Intellectual "head trips" are not enough to do this. We must recreate the entire encoding of the crystal and thus release the emotionality with the associated word patterns and sensory experience with the transmuting power of enthusiasm, and then at the same time release all cause, effect, record and memory with the continued use of the Violet Flame which is the transmuting power which purifies the mental body which in turn has its effect positively and powerfully felt on the emotional and physical bodies. Think of the mental body encompassing the emotional and physical bodies, Think of the emotional body encompassing the physical body. Think of the concept of permeation when thinking of the idea of encompassment. Think of the emotional body encompassing and permeating the physical body and extending beyond it as the mental body encompasses and permeates the emotions I and physical bodies and extends beyond them. One then sees that they are not separated but are interlocked or interwoven. We cannot affect the mental body without affecting the emotional and physical bodies, We cannot affect the emotional body without affecting the physical, and as long as we are identified with the physical body the reverse holds true. The physical body is the doorway to the emotional and mental bodies and it must be operating obediently in accord with physical laws to help the crystals dissolve not only in the physical body but in the surrounding environment by the Law of Right Action, that the crystals, both physically and environmentally, then can yield up the encoded messages and the emotional and mental bodies can therefore be accessed in turn." JWR

On the Table- Being the Pointholdee

This is where the inner essence is viewed and transmutation practiced and applied. Thought (sensory memory), emotionality and word pattern, with Unconditional Love and Forgiveness moves one upscale within the emotional body. 7x7

During a pointholding session the pressure/stimuli assists to open the crystalline formations that are holding the memory. Facilitation aids in the ability to access our unique past. It is our 'job' as a pointholdee to find what's there, and work with what comes forth. Being perfectly still and breathing deep and regular are the first principles to apply. (if we are on the table we are already nutritionally prepared).

Intensifying and encompassing the 3 creative energies of emotion, word pattern, and sensory memory (the result of thought) with Unconditional Love and Forgiveness leads to consciousness change.

Physical sensations we may feel while on the table (and as a pointholder) range from numbness, electricity, throbbing, aching, pain, vibrations, heat and cold to varying degrees. When we feel these sensations we intensify them to get to the fullness of memory, emotion and words.

"Redefine your relationship with pain." I still hear Doug's voice reminding me. Rejoice in the pain! Enthusiastically feel it with Love and allow it to release. Life can be a pointholding session, when we have the commitment to see, feel and find the words associated in the moment of resistance. As we become aware of opportunities to transmute in daily lives (they are all around us), in this way we can also transmute/change consciousness. Make private time each day for inner work.

As self-responsibility increases, we get to a place where we can 'work' internally on releasing patterns of resistance as they are presented in daily life. See daily experience as an opportunity to apply principles. Lovingly and willing endure all things is a great place to start.

As we inevitably (with commitment and perseverance) move up the scale of emotions, we will begin to discover more and more parts of our self we were previously unaware of, this is the point. We find more of the SENSORY MEMORY/ WORD PATTERN/EMOTIONALTY that had been stored in the unconscious. This eventually results in becoming aware of the pain stored in the bodies, physical, emotional, mental and spiritual. The required willingness to re-experience and release increases, as one goes upscale through all the bodies in reverse order It is important to go within, study and prepare through meditation, stillness and breath.

Check in with your self while on the table (or off). Am I willing for the pain to increase (physical, emotional, mental), last as long as necessary, forever?

Access Forgiveness…. It's not as simple as saying you are sorry…true repentance, requires FEELING, really feeling forgiveness to the self…unconditionally. This takes practice in my experience.

Feel Love. Enthusiastically feel.

Gratitude can be expressed in words, but without feeling the words are empty.

Practice feeling Forgiveness, Love, Gratitude, and it will make it much easier to access when on the table, sometimes during excruciating burning searing pain.

"May the burning fire of the kundalini purify every vestige of blocked activity that the soul may return to it capacity to choose oneness with the creator" JWR

Checklist prior to Pointholding;

1. Nails trimmed and filed
2. Pillows/chairs etc. required
3. Decision for points to hold
4. Group decision of facilitator (usually pointholder nearest to the head of the pointholdee)
5. Ask for loving guidance.

The suppressed enthusiasm, pain, anger, fear, grief, apathy and unconsciousness exists within- being held in the crystalline structure wholistically- spiritual, mental emotional and physical.

Pointholding allows the crystal to begin to be dissolved, which is the 'computer chip' holding the resisted past in a constant state of creation.

Pointholding does not cause pain (further trauma), we hold the points with continuous focused pressure to unlock/release the pain which is already present.

Directional change without disconnecting from the point often assists the pointholdee to access more.

To summarize, some of the principles to apply are;

- Do not give anyone any more pressure than the pointholdee can lovingly and willingly endure~
- Communicate!

- When in doubt, DON'T!
- Hold the points with focus, staying on the point until the session is complete.
- When our fingers become numb, and we can't feel where we are on the point, use vision to make sure you are on the point.
- Maintain as much continuous pressure as possible.
- The person on the table is responsible for communicating more or less pressure, with that said, a facilitator may check with the pointholdee from time to time and ask.
- A directional change without coming off the point is often sufficient to allow more to be accessed.
- Having attachment/non attachment to outcome, goals, ideas about healing, etc. can greatly inhibit/assist the session.
- Common sensations occur for the pointholder. These include numbness, heat, electricity, pain and throbbing to varying degrees. See How We Heal pg.257

What we resist persists~

Resistances made manifest~
There are three main ways we may see our resistance patterns reflected to us by our environment. When we feel an emotional response/reactive trigger we may observe the external pattern as the same reactive 'position' we hold, the opposite of what we are holding, or we may hold the minutest amount of same, still in the area of honest observation, or a combination of the above.

All are opportunities to apply the laws of Unconditional Love and Forgiveness if we choose.

We become more and more aware of our patterns of behavior. This allows greater responsibility (ability to respond appropriately).

Be very aware when you get triggered emotions. By projecting emotion attached to resistance into the environment, we miss the opportunity to contain (control) and transmute. If this happens forgive yourself, and know another opportunity (trigger) will come. With disciplined effort it gets easier to see the opportunities as they present themselves, and accessing forgiveness and love becomes a natural part of the process. When we do not miss these opportunities, and recognize the pattern with the emotional quality, while lovingly and willingly enduring (actively), the transmutation is taking place within and the change is reflected in the outer condition.

- Self responsibility (owning your pattern and emotion). Justification becomes less and less.

In summation, our resistance patterns fit perfectly with our environment, by the law of attraction until we first become aware of it, then choose to change it.
This is done upon the application of principles.

Facilitation

Again, this is an increasingly intuitive process. The further upscale we go on the emotional tone scale, the greater the intuition is opened and available.
The facilitator is a guide, the transmutation (work) is being done as an internal process within the person on the table- pointholdee. As we are gaining in self - responsibility, the 'need' for external assistance diminishes.
One responsibility of the facilitator is to keep the person breathing deep and regular (no pausing between

breaths), and holding the body perfectly still. Gentle reminders are usually enough, intuition rules. Sometimes I speak softly, sometimes loudly if the person is really foggy, and requires this. Watch for your own resistance patterns here regarding communication. Mastering physical discipline of breathing and being still leads to the access of the emotional body.

Facilitating requires focus, without involvement. In other words, what the person is going through on the table is their process, be there for that person to the best of current ability to do so. The facilitator doesn't require the story of what's going on. It is entirely up to the pointholdee how much is shared. The focus is on finding and maintaining the word patterns, emotion and sensory memory, putting them together simultaneously, and accessing/applying the Power of Gratitude, Love and Forgiveness (the three powers). As you practice B.E., you will find your intuition gradually returning. As a result you often see, feel and hear what the person on the table is experiencing sometimes before they do. We do not hurry or make suggestions. The joy of self-discovery is very important. It's up to us, when we are on the table to find and transmute. Again the facilitator is nothing more than a guide.

We do not ask 'why' during facilitation, as 'why' brings the focus to an intellectual one, which is sidetracking the process.

Be aware of our own communication resistance while facilitating, and begin to change them. If you have a pattern of being afraid to speak, for example, recognize this as an opportunity to change this. Speak up. Likewise, if it's your pattern to compulsively speak, then take a breath before speaking and ask yourself what to say that is appropriate-responsible in the moment.

We do not share what happens on the table with anyone else without the consent of that person. Common questions/comments as a facilitator are;

- 'what's happening now?'
- 'where are you?'
- 'can you find a time you felt this way before?'
- 'intensify that'.

When you hear a pointholdee talking in past tense, this is telling a story, this is not the experience, remind the person to 'be there now'. This sounds like a contradiction, yet we bring the past into the now where the resistance may be released.

If a person is observing their memory like watching a movie, it is of utmost importance that they get in their body within the memory. We say something like, 'ok, you've got the memory, now get in your body and experience it from there'.

Often we leave our bodies during trauma, a defense mechanism employed during an experience that was 'too much' to experience in the moment. Getting back into the body is a step toward willingness of re-experience, required for release.

"Lovingly and willingly endure ALL things".

Word Patterns

Word patterns are the words encoded within the crystal, most often, simple and short.

When found, we begin by intensifying externally increasing volume if necessary. It usually requires persistent external expression, to increase intensity.

When the outward expression (venting) has completed, then repeat internally intensifying by containing.

Affirmations/decrees are not word patterns.

In fact this adds another layer to undo. If the pointholdee is speaking what is considered an affirmation, such as 'I am a being of light'…this is blocking the process of transmutation, by overlaying (like putting a wet blanket on a fire) upon that which is to come forth and be released.

Feel WHAT you feel WITH love simultaneously.

Feel Love while feeling angry for example.

Honesty to one's self is increasingly required.

Again, guide the person in finding the word pattern.

 If a person is saying 'I'm angry, or I'm scared..etc., this is a description of emotion, not the word pattern, so a facilitator will say something like 'intensify the feeling and look for the words', or 'Ok you got the feeling, now find the words' then when the pointholdee has found the word pattern, such as…."leave me alone", the facilitator will guide by saying, 'now put the feeling into the words'…..'are you in the memory?'. Remember you are guiding the pointholdee to keep what they've found and find the rest, until they have all three simultaneously- word pattern, sensory memory and emotionality.

Expand/Intensify from there, and transmute.

At this point the facilitator may ask, 'is there something about this you can love?'. If the answer is no, then 'what do you really feel?', "intensify that", the person can feel disappointed they feel angry, or embarrassed/ashamed.

This is felt and released (feel WHAT you feel with Love) to get to the underlying emotion, this is called resistance to the resistance.

Be willing as facilitator's to make mistakes.

As we gain experience on the table this also improves our skills at being effective facilitator's.

Sexual Energy

Upon activation of the Healing Crisis at the level of unconsciousness (where HC begins) hyperactivity of the gonads occurs. Remember this occurs in unconsciousness at every new level of emotion in the seven times seven. With each level the awareness increases.

The hyperactivity of unconsciousness may be experienced as sexual stimulation. At this time of hormonal stimulation it is important to remember the lymphatic enzymes. See HWH

Acknowledge the H.C. in unconsciousness/gonads the same as when we have hyperactivity of the thyroid/anger or any other emotion, we remind ourselves of the H.C. in the moment as it is happening, and we catch it (apply transmutation) before projecting it outward. There will be a relative level of balance experienced from a more sensitive perspective after the Healing Crisis has been worked with. Individually and collectively we hold sexual trauma. It is prudent to work with the associated memory, words and emotion related to our sexuality.

When it comes to sexual energy, because of the strong magnetic force (unconscious desire to procreate) combined with the unconscious layers of resistance. We can sometimes forget that it is a Healing Crisis, and seek to involve another.

Over the years I have practiced methods of moving the sexual energy with breath, while working through layers of emotional/mental patterns involved.

This assists in an expanding awareness and release of emotional resistance that is held in regards to sexuality Stored potentialities of creation are present within the fluids and complex energetic composition of Sexual Energy.

Natural Beauty

In recent years an increase has occurred in many forms of augmenting the physicality. Teeth whitening (proven to cause oral cancers), breast implants, botox (and other forms of nerve toxins injected for wrinkle reduction), tanning, facial reconstruction, lipo suction etc. etc.-

The healing crisis requires we go back through the way we came, undoing suppression physically, emotionally, mentally and spiritually. For this reason remaining as natural and using natural products is recommended.

Be Beauty, from the inside out.

Iridology-Sclerology

By familiarizing ourselves with the study of the iris and sclera, we have another tool to guide us toward nutritional necessity, pointholding priorities, genetic overlays, and consciousness change as it is reflected in the eyes. Making recommendations by evaluating the iris/sclera requires intense study and application over many years. The more we know, the more we realize we don't know applies here. A self-examination mirror is effective in monitoring our own eyes.

See HWH for basic eye charts.

➢Biological Transmutations
(How We Heal pg. 376)

➢Sympathy vs. Empathy- (How We Heal pg. 316)

Holding the Light

As we progress upscale releasing resistance, the awareness (new level of light- vibration) that is now present must be consciously maintained, particularly in the beginning of change. Being aware when old habits/patterns present themselves, we are given opportunity to see and consciously maintain the newly acquired freedom. Simply by not repeated the old pattern. When we miss it or choose to repeat old habits forgive one's self, have a laugh and carry on- onward and upward.

Justification-Purification-Sanctification

➢ LIS-Book One, pg. 204-208

'The secret is to be without effort, to do without trying, to see without focus, to have
without owning, and to express without necessity. Such is the realm of the masters.' JWR

As we transmute the emotional/mental body's we experience natural opening's where inner vision- clairvoyance, inner auditory- clairaudience, telepathy- morphogenic communication, inner knowing-clairsentience. These are natural spiritual qualities that unfold as the endocrine system heals (pineal).

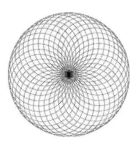

Sunset-Sunrise~ Moonrise-Moonset-Stargazing

Spending time in concentrated gratitude.

Limit unnatural light- get a sufficient amount of natural light daily.
Music!
Listening to live music, and making music!

Dance~
Sing~
Celebrate~

Fasting

One day low sugar vegetable juice fasting (celery, parsley, etc.) can assist cleansing and alkalize. A 1-3 day watermelon juice fast with water in addition or fasting from substances we know are not supportive to health. A long term fast, more than three days is a spiritual calling. Fasting causes a toxic dump into the bloodstream, and must be carefully considered and prepared for properly. Sufficient water to flush toxins is paramount.

Stones~ Crystals

The five platonic solids make an interesting study.
I listen to my intuition in regards to wearing stones, and having them in my environment. They are alive with concentrated consciousness- history.
Some Stones are best left where they belong, such as lava.
Each person has a unique experience/assistance from the complex structures of stones.
Again, ask and you shall receive.

Essential Oils~ Burning Scents

Essential oils are part of my daily support, particularly for the emotional body. In the bath, fragrance has assisted me through many a healing crisis.

Flat white Sage leaf, flat leaf Cedar, Sweetgrass, and Tobacco- the four sacred herbs in First Nations of Turtle Island. They assist to remind to be in Gratitude, Love and Prayer within our daily walk.

Water- Sun- Air- Earth

A simple daily routine, naturally provides support and healing. Sunbathing- every person's skin is unique- and the sun is different each day. Consider.
Air bathing- may be incorporated with a brisk brushing massage. Bathing- Essential oils such as Tulsi (holy basil), baking soda and good quality salt.
Lakes, Oceans, Rivers and Hot Springs. Immersing the feet in water, on the grass, sand etc. Simply taking a walk in a natural environment, going for a swim, observing the plants, animals, birds and trees, may greatly assist the process of the H.C.~

Body Electronics Pointholding Intensives

See website for scheduled events.
When practicing B.E., this book will serve as a guide
and provide the flow sheet for your records.

Visualization and Consciousness Course

In 2005 a V&C was held by Douglas Morrison. It was
four weeks in duration. This is advanced work attended
by Certified B.E. Instructor's.

*IT WOULD BE WISE TO REMEMBER THAT
THERE ARE DUALITIES WHICH ARE BASED ON
DUALITIES WHICH IN TURN ARE BASED ON
EVEN MORE SUBTLE DUALITIES UNTIL WE
REACH THE SERIES OF BASIC TRUTH-
RESISTED TRUTH DUALITIES WHICH BIND US
TO THE ACTIVITIES IN THE PHYSICAL WORLD.
AS THE TRUTH-RESISTED TRUTH DUALITIES
ARE INDIVIDUALLY EXPERIENCED ONE
SHALL THEN EXPERIENCE THE TIME -SPACE-
CONTINUUM- JWR*

Illia Heart~ Brief Biography

Raised on a farm near the shores of Lake Huron, Illia enjoyed a rural childhood. In her twenties, (1980's) she travelled to western Canada. There she met Kalu Rinpoche on Mt. Tuam, Salt Spring Island, B.C. in 1986. Illia owned and operated a health food store, a bookstore as well as a 'Wholistic Health Centre' from 1993- 2008.

From 1988-1997 she participated with a Bhakti Yoga Ashram devoted to practicing the Kriya teachings given by Mahavatar Babaji, that were passed through Lahiri Mahasaya, Sri Yukteswar, and Paramahansa Yogananda. During this time Illia earned a degree in Ayurveda, and taught numerous workshops on Yogic and Ayurvedic principles and practices in Toronto Canada.

In 1999 Illia began several years of study and practical application of Body Electronics. Under the instruction of Douglas Morrison, she attended two complete Instructor's Courses- 2003 and '04, as well as the Visualization and Consciousness course in 2005. Eventually Illia taught alongside Douglas Morrison. In total Illia participated in over 50 weeks of B.E. Pointholding Intensives with Dr. Morrison.

Illia spent over ten years of self- discovery with Drunvalo Melchizedek. She travelled to Peru with Drunvalo participating in ceremony in honour of the Condor and the Eagle prophesy. Drunvalo certified her as a teacher of his work, Awakening the Illuminated Heart in 2011.

Currently Illia owns and operates a shop in Ganges, Salt Spring Island, B.C., Canada- Illia's- Body- Mind- Spirit. She holds Body Electronics Intensives and workshops on wholistic health.

"All comes into natural harmony in the presence of Love"

Illia~

Made in the USA
Columbia, SC
26 April 2018